A Merrow Monograph

PHYSIOLOGY AND HYGIENE
OF
MATERIALS AND CLOTHING

Merrow Monographs

General Editor: J. Gordon Cook, B.SC., PH.D., F.R.I.C.

Concise, authoritative reviews of technical topics.

Textile Technology Series

PHYSIOLOGY AND HYGIENE OF MATERIALS AND CLOTHING

E. T. Renbourn, B.Sc., M.D., M.R.C.P.
St. Catherine's, Frimley, Surrey

MERROW

Merrow Publishing Co. Ltd.
276 Hempstead Road
Watford   Herts   England

© 1971 *Merrow Publishing Co. Ltd.*

ISBN 0 900 54112 1 Clothbound
ISBN 0 900 54113 X Paperback

Printed in Great Britain at the Pitman Press, Bath

CONTENTS

ACKNOWLEDGEMENT

The author and publishers would like to thank the Editors of CIBA Review, who kindly permitted them to make use of information and illustrations from CIBA Review 1964/4.

1

INTRODUCTION

The origin of clothing is wrapped in obscurity, but the first garments were undoubtedly derived from animal skins or vegetation which were readily obtainable. It is probable that the original purpose of these garments was to provide protection from the elements. An important factor in their evolution, however, may have been fear of the unknown which necessitated protection of the sexual organs from magical influences. This may be the origin of the primitive hip girdle associated with prehistoric statues of Venus. Such a girdle was used by the servant women of ancient Egypt; it is found even today amongst primitive African people. From the girdle hung a protective genital curtain, ornaments and objects of utility. The association between modesty and clothing was a later innovation which was probably connected with the rise of religious beliefs. Clothing also hid from public gaze that which was considered unaesthetic.

Throughout human history, there has been a preoccupation with keeping the body unduly warm, rather than maintaining it comfortably cool. An ancient Greek doctrine insisted that, for the requirements of health, air must pass into the body through the invisible pores of the skin, and the insensible humours of the body must be able to pass out freely. It was this "breathing" of the skin which required that the body should be kept continuously warm. Cold air and strong emotions blocked the exit of the humours of the body in the form of the "insensibilis perspiratio" of the skin, and forced them back to the internal organs. Inflammation and disease ensued, the pent-up humours pouring out through the nose, lungs, bowels and kidneys. Even today grand-mothers may speak with bated breath of the dangers of rashes "being struck inwardly" by a draught of cold air.

As a consequence of this doctrine, the body has for centuries been smothered with clothing and particularly wool, a condition often regarded as a panacea for health. Nevertheless, Seneca, the Greek philosopher, delared that it was the very man who sheltered himself unduly from the cold who ran the greatest risk of being chilled by the gentlest breeze.

At the turn of the present century, the flannel rash—a combination of a sweat rash and a mild fungus disorder of the skin—was very common in people who wore an over-abundance of thick flannel underclothes. Nowadays, such a condition is rarely seen by doctors. Until the First World War, it was not uncommon for people, especially children, to be dressed in winter "like an onion". Six layers or more of clothing enveloped the human trunk, many of the garments being of flannel or its cotton imitation, flannelette. Children of the poorer classes were sometimes sewn into their under-clothes for the duration of the cold season.

In 1914, a Doctor Fitz of Boston circulated to a hundred well-known physicians a questionnaire relating to the use of clothing fabrics in health and disease. The replies displayed markedly conflicting opinions amongst his colleagues. This, said Dr. Fitz, was related to the general ignorance of textile science and clothing hygiene. Since then much has been learned, but physicians and even textile experts are still largely ignorant about some of the fundamental aspects of clothing physiology and hygiene.

2

THE BODY UNDER THE CLOTHING

Temperature

The temperature of either the exposed or the clothed skin varies widely from one part of the body to another under conditions of comfort; only when the body is warm is the skin temperature at all uniform. It is often said that the temperature of the healthy body (in the mouth or rectum) is constant within narrow limits. In most people, however, there is a diurnal variation of 2–3°F (1·2–1·8°C) or more, the highest temperatures being in the evening. Within a quarter hour or so of a hot bath or violent exercise, the body temperature may rise to 103°F (39·4°C). There is a seasonal variation of body temperature of 1–2°F, even in Europe, and this is more marked in the tropics. Furthermore, it is not generally realized that in perfectly normal people, apprehension—for instance, on the first day of going to school or of being the subject of an experiment—may raise the body temperature to 100°F (37·8°C) or more. Such physiological and psychological increases in temperature are due to a purposive change in the setting of the body "thermostat", rather than to heat accumulation arising from an inability to lose heat efficiently. Clothing plays little or no role in these normal variations in body temperature. Nudists have more or less the same body temperature as people who are fully dressed.

The body can be regarded as an internal combustion engine producing, at rest, about 80 kilocalories (90 watts) an hour in a healthy adult; 4–5 times as much, or more, is produced with strenuous exercise. In a temperate climate, the resting internal body temperature is maintained between about

96–99°F (35·6–37·2°C) by the "thermostat" at the base of the brain; this maintains a balance between heat production and heat loss. About one quarter of the body heat is dissipated at the body surface as latent heat derived from the water vapour—insensible perspiration—which is continually passing out through the skin; the rest of the heat is lost by radiation and convection at the surface of the clothing. Under ordinary conditions, heat loss by conduction, except that from the feet, is unimportant. The body adapts itself to warm conditions, such as sunlight, warm air or additional clothing; partly by opening up its "hot water pipes"—the skin blood vessels—so that more heat can be lost by convection and radiation, and partly by an automatic increase in the amount of insensible perspiration liberated.

With the above reservations, it may be said that the body maintains its internal temperature at a reasonably steady level. Under conditions of heavy work, or when the outside temperature rises to over 80°F (26·5°C), the minute coil glands of the skin begin to pour out a dilute salt solution, the liquid sweat. When this evaporates at the skin level or within the clothing, much more heat is lost as latent heat, and the skin surface reaches a fairly stable temperature level. Thus, the body can adapt itself, within limits, to environmental warmth and to more or to less clothing.

The artist's model and the nudist are prepared to go without clothing at an air temperature between say 55–70°F (12·8–21°C). Given an opportunity to adapt, most people on a beach will feel quite comfortable at the upper level of this temperature range. When a person is nude under such conditions, the skin of the trunk is cooler and that of the limbs is warmer than when clothing is worn; despite this, the average skin temperature is not greatly affected.

The health-giving value of sunlight on the exposed skin is not only physiological but also psychological. Furthermore, a gentle breeze playing over the nude skin tones up the underlying muscles by causing a reflex tightening; this, together with cutaneous and mental stimulation, is the basis of the

4

Fig. 1. Bark cloth aprons held by plaited belts are the only clothing worn by these natives from Hansa Bay, New Guinea.
(*Photo by courtesy of the Ethnological Museum, Basle*)

invigoration felt when the clothes are removed. In a similar way, air movement over the body occurring under loose, light and ventilated clothing acts as a mild physiological stimulus, encouraging a healthful condition of the skin.

Chilling

It is now known that undue chilling of the body by cold air or wet clothing cannot obstruct the passage of insensible perspiration through the skin. The usual explanation of the effects of chilling is that it is followed by reflex closing-up of the blood vessels in the organs (tonsils, lungs, kidneys, etc.), thus allowing pathogenic organisms in the blood to establish a foothold. However, this simple explanation is now held in doubt, as there is evidence that severe chilling may act as a "stress" agent and impair the protective functions of the suprarenal glands.

Closing up the skin blood vessels, with consequent cooling of the skin, also occurs as an adaptive process at the commencement of certain fevers. This explains why a person with an impending cold, pneumonia or malaria, etc., despite being warmly clad and with a rising internal temperature, will be the only one in a room to complain of the slightest draught.

Sudden cold or emotion causes goose skin, a remnant of the hair-raising reflex of animals; by roughening the skin surface, the body may increase its boundary layer of relatively still air.

Fig. 2. This allegorical representation of spring by Sandro Botticelli (1444/5–1510) depicts the flat chest and protruding lower abdomen of the female figure apparently considered ideal in the period following the Middle Ages.

(*Photo: Alinari, courtesy of the Galleria Antica e Moderna, Florence*)

Fig. 3. The first historical evidence of corset-like waist constriction, this ivory and gold 'snake goddess' from Minoan Crete dates back to the 16th century B.C.

(*Photo by courtesy of the Museum of Fine Arts, Boston*)

3

METHODOLOGY IN CLOTHING PHYSIOLOGY

There are cardinal principles to be remembered in the physiological assessment of clothing properties. No two people are similar in their likes or dislikes or in their physiological response to clothing, and it may be unwise to draw conclusions from even the most elaborate experiments carried out on a single "guinea pig". Insufficient is yet known of the significance of absolute physiological levels; *differences* in measurement—viz. in body temperature and pulse rate—are more meaningful. As few standards are available, it is wiser to compare the characteristics of an existing garment with that of a new one.

In general, research starts at the "bench level" using a physical model (e.g. measurements of thermal insulation, air-, wind-, vapour- or water-transmission of a sample of fabric); this is followed by closely-controlled physiological experiments in a climatic chamber and, finally, assessment in the field.

It is essential to carry out experiments on clothing systems worn by human beings under appropriate conditions. The main virtue of the climatic chamber lies in its controlled environment, but the characteristics of desert, jungle, temperate or cold climates are much more than hot, damp, cold or moving air. Solar radiation, hot desert sand, the jungle flora or fauna, rain or snow are not easily reproduced in a climatic chamber. The climatic chamber has, nevertheless, a screening value.

Physiological differences between garments worn by a man resting horizontally may increase, decrease, or change in

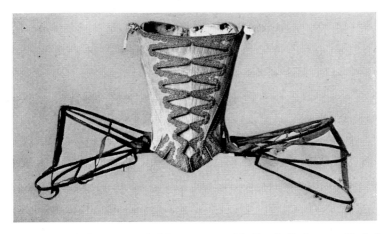

Fig. 4. An 18th century whalebone corset with "poches" for an elliptical farthingale.

(Photo by courtesy of the Bavarian National Museum, Munich)

direction when he is up and physically active. The properties of any item of clothing are modified by what lies above and below. Thus, the properties of a sock or stocking are modified by shoes or boots; those of the underclothes are modified by the outer garments; all may be modified by a soldier's equipment and by the load on his back. For this reason, all clothing must be assessed as an indivisible, physiological system.

For the reasons given above, clothing experiments should be of a comparative nature and should be carried out on *groups* of subjects. In order to minimize the sources of physiological variation, statistical design of experiment is necessary, generally in the form of randomised blocks. Efficient design of experiment is even more important than the analysis of resulting data. Variance or co-variance techniques minimize the effect of differences between subjects and differences due to physiological and psychological acclimatization—to the garments, to the ambient environment and to other conditions of exposure. Because of the marked variability between

9

*Fig. 5. This mosaic from Pella, probably dating from the 4th century B.C.,
shows Alexander the Great and his friend Krateros attacking a lion. The naked
human body inspired the sculptural masterpieces of Ancient Greece and was also
not associated with any inhibitions in neighbouring Macedonia.*

(*Photo by courtesy of the Musée archéologique, Salonika*)

human subjects and the relatively large errors inherent in
biological methods, significant differences in physiological
measurements may still arise from chance factors. A similar
statistical approach should, of course, be used in the textile
laboratory.

It is clear that measurements of garment, skin and internal
body temperatures form an integral part of clothing studies.
These measurements are made by using suitable thermocouples or thermistors. The radiometer does not lend itself to
use under clothing, but it has proved useful in assessing the
sites of heat loss in cold weather garments. Pulse rate, energy
output and sweat loss are useful in measuring the effects of
garments on men working or exercising under various

environmental conditions. A great deal of research has gone into the measurement of vapour pressure gradients between clothing layers, but results have not, as yet, been very successful. The weight of clothing before and after an experiment throws useful light on the hydrokinetic properties of garments. In the climatic chamber, men would be resting, walking or carrying out some form of work activity.

Assessment in the Field

The next phase of the research is carried out in a realistic climatic environment. The team physicist takes on the added duties of meteorologist. His instruments are sited in the open, or are sheltered in a tent or hut. Physiological methods must be simplified for field use, and automatic and telemetric techniques have become of great value. A statistical approach is used in the field, as in the laboratory.

Physiological measurements, individually or collectively, are valuable as indices of discomfort or bodily strain, but they do not necessarily indicate what the sportsman, worker, soldier, explorer or astronaut can perform under operational conditions when wearing a particular clothing system. For this reason, it is expedient to carry out *performance tests*, the best of these being realistic activities. For the soldier, the latter may take the form of accuracy of firing, speed of digging a standard trench, efficiency in assembling a weapon or in taking a carburetter to pieces (e.g. when wearing cold-weather gloves). Suitable performance tests could be devised for any work situation.

Subjective assessment of the effects of clothing is carried out in two phases. During the replicate periods of a designed experiment, men will be given a simple questionnaire such as: "Are you comfortable, cold or very cold?"; "Is your skin dry, sweaty or very sweaty?"; "Are you rested, tired or exhausted?" and so forth. Since the garments are not mentioned, subjective bias is minimized. Questionnaires of this sort must be carefully designed, and the results analysed by

11

non-parametric, statistical techniques. It is, of course, important that the subjects do not know the nature of the experimental garments they are wearing, as this itself might lead to subjective bias. At the end of the experiment, the men will be asked which of the garments—hats, gloves, boots, suits or underwear etc.—they prefer, and the reasons for their preference. The results of such a preference questionnaire must, however, be examined with caution; men and women are often prepared to give answers on matters of which they have little or no experience. They are, naturally, more concerned with the *handle* or appearance of a garment than with its more important functional qualities. Their opinions may be swayed by a dominant personality. Acceptance of a new design may be modified by psychological factors. In women, fashion will often play a dominant role.

Clothing and the Clinician

An examination of clothing may be of help to the clinician. Badly-fitting clothing, for example, in an adult may suggest a marked recent change in body weight. Unexpectedly odd clothing, or dirty clothing, are characteristic of the lax habits of the tramp or the drug addict; they may suggest the presence of mental disease. An ammoniacal smell from the underclothes will indicate chronic urinary obstruction and infection. In an elderly man, white stains on the shoes may be a result of diabetes mellitus. A very tight collar may induce fainting attacks, and constriction by garters or a modern pantie-girdle can aggravate chilblains and varicose veins. In cold weather, short skirts and thin nylon stockings may be contributory factors in the "mini-skirt syndrome"—or erythrocyanosis crurum.

4

AERODYNAMICS OF CLOTHING

Air, Wind and Warmth

The so-called "warmth" of clothing materials is due only in small measure to the insulating properties of the fibres themselves; it results mainly from the high thermal insulation of air trapped between the yarns and fibres. All surfaces, particularly those which are rough or fibrous, tend to cling to air by "aerodynamic drag". Because of convective heat currents which normally pass out from the warm skin through the clothing, the boundary layer of air clinging to the skin and to clothing fabrics is in a state of slight movement. This applies not only to air in contact with the two exposed faces of a fabric but to that in contact with the enormous surface area associated with the interior yarns and their constituent fibres. Most clothing fabrics contain about 70 per cent of air by volume; in a wool blanket, this may be as high as 90 per cent. A hairy fabric entraps more air than a smooth one. The transitory "cool" or "warm" feel we experience when a fabric touches the skin relates largely to the nature of the fabric surface, which may be smooth or hairy. It has little connection with the true thermal insulation characteristics of the fabric as a whole.

Although the thermal insulative property of different fibres varies appreciably, this is of little significance due to the much greater effect of air trapped within and between the yarns of fabrics. In general, the nature of the fibre surface and of the weave construction play only minor roles in thermal insulation, the most important single factor being the fabric thickness. This was demonstrated by Rubner before the present century. Thus, to say that wool is warmer than cotton can be meaningless, because wool does not easily lend itself to the production of very thin fabrics. It is, furthermore, difficult to measure the thickness of a hairy fabric accurately without causing some compression, which changes the functional thickness and, hence, the warmth. In the case of blankets, these are placed on top of the body and thus exposed only to slight pressure.

Humidity has only a negligible effect on the thermal insulation properties of air; in other words, damp air has about the same "warmth" value as dry air.

In the textile laboratory, the thermal insulation characteristics of a fabric are commonly measured by assessing the heat flow through a sample placed on a horizontal copper plate, the temperature of the plate being maintained constant by a variable electric input. Part of the thermal insulation value (the "tog" value of Rees) is due to the layer of air between the fabric and the plate. Thus, a crinkled piece of paper or plastic sheeting gives a higher "tog" value than a similar piece laid smoothly on the plate. Likewise, a crepe, a pile or a terry surface increases the functional thickness and hence the thermal insulation value. Tramps have long appreciated the warmth of many layers of crinkled newspaper. Clothes are generally worn vertically—not horizontally —and the air spaces between a number of vertical garment layers cannot be imitated by the horizontal plate technique.

Insulation of a Cylindrical Body

When an insulating layer is placed over a narrow cylinder (rather than a plate), the thickness-warmth relationship of fabrics no longer strictly holds. Addition of the insulating layer increases the exposed surface area through which heat loss takes place. Several inches of clothing may be built up, layer by layer, over the cylindrical trunk of the body to increase the thermal insulation, but each layer of a given thickness adds less warmth than the one beneath. Engineers

14

Fig. 6. The tight swaddling of infants was declared by physicians to be dangerous to health as early as the 18th century. This painting from the old Paris Orphanage shows abandoned children committed to the care of St. Vincent de Paul.

(*Photo by courtesy of the Musée de l'Assistance Publique, Paris*)

have long understood the difficulties in thermally insulating narrow pipes of a diameter, for example, corresponding to that of a human finger. The thermal insulation value of a glove material is limited; a thickness of more than about a quarter inch will not only keep the fingers separated and impair dexterity, but it may permit more heat to be lost through the added surface area than is retained by the insulative material.

Wind

Wind is a factor which modifies the thermal insulation value and hence the warmth of clothing fabrics. The body in movement produces its own breeze; under certain circumstances, e.g. when skiing or travelling in an open vehicle, this may become an appreciable wind. By removing the relatively motionless insulating air layers on the outer surface and fabric interior, the wind may impair the intrinsic thermal insulation properties of the clothing. Although good wind-resistance is a characteristic of thin, tight-weave fabrics, the same effect can be achieved by two relatively open-weave materials used one over the other. The effect may be compared with the wind-breaking characteristics of an ordinary hedge. Mosquito netting, in the same way, will reduce the cooling effect of a fan.

Leather

It is often claimed that leather "breathes", a belief that may derive from the erroneous idea that living skin is an organ of respiration. The laboratory test of breathing, like the measurement of air permeability of a fabric, depends upon the passage of air through leather under a pressure differential. However, under realistic conditions, the opportunity for air to pass through leather may be greatly restricted. Such conditions may apply, for example, in a shoe when walking, when the amount of air passing through a dense leather sole, or a leather upper, particularly if dubbined, waxed or polished daily, must be relatively small. Leather is, however, fairly permeable to water vapour.

Tight Clothing and Air Layers

The optimum thickness of an insulating, inter-garment air layer is about one quarter inch; at greater thicknesses convection effects begin to play a significant role. If a thin garment is placed within such an air space of optimum thickness—which is substantially thicker than most clothing fabrics—it is unlikely to increase appreciably the total thermal insulation; it would do so, however, where the air spaces are larger, e.g. between the trousers and the leg, or under a skirt. This accounts for the effectiveness of pyjama trousers worn beneath ski slacks under cold conditions.

Some years ago, the author carried out an experiment to examine the effect on body temperature of wearing (*a*) a cotton vest, (*b*) a soft string vest, and (*c*) no vest at all. Three groups of soldiers were dressed accordingly, all other clothing worn being identical. They carried out standard exercises in summer weather in England, bearing a standard pack on the back. Surprisingly, no statistically significant differences could be found in skin or deep body temperatures of soldiers in the three groups.

This "missing vest" phenomenon may be explained by the presence of an air layer of optimum thickness beneath the shirt. It is apparent that, under certain circumstances, the air layers between fabrics may be more important than the fabrics themselves. Other physical factors must, of course, be considered.

Tight-fitting outer garments decrease skin ventilation and, by reducing the thickness of the air layers between garments, will minimize the total thermal insulation of the clothing system. This becomes important under conditions of severe cold; tight-fitting clothing then becomes cold clothing. A wind-break garment should fit the body fairly well, its waist and lower border fitting snugly, otherwise cold air may be sucked in around the lower edge to cause a ballooning effect at the back; this is commonly seen when a skier is moving rapidly down a slope or a motor cyclist is travelling fast. In the same way, a belt worn around tropical garments (bush jacket or trousers) diminishes cooling by "chimney ventilation".

Tight stocks have long disappeared from military uniforms. Even a tight-fitting collar, however, may bring about a fainting attack by pressing on a hypersensitive carotid artery in the neck. In the past, rigid, over-tight corsets were said to cause deformity of the chest, and even of the liver. Tight garters have now gone out of fashion.

Elastic, synthetic-fibre stockings are of value in sustaining a sluggish circulation. An elastic garment which is worn too tight around the thigh, however, may restrict the circulation in the legs; this causes the swelling of the ankles described by physicians as the "pantie-girdle syndrome".

5

HYDROKINETICS OF CLOTHING SYSTEMS

Clothing and Static Electricity

Fibres which absorb only a very small quantity of moisture (e.g. many synthetics, cellulose triacetate etc.) tend to produce, by inter-clothing or clothing-body friction, sufficient electrostatic charge to cause noticeable crackling or sparking. Static electricity has caused difficulties in the opening of parachutes; it makes thin synthetic fibre garments adhere one to another, and may be responsible for the riding-up of clothing during body movement. The soiling of synthetic fibre garments is influenced by the production of electro-static charges. The generation of electrostatic charges in the dry atmosphere of heated operating theatres has, in the past, caused the explosion of anaesthetics mixed with air or oxygen.

Special anti-static finishing agents, and the use of con-ducting fibres and yarns, have done much to eliminate the difficulties caused by electrostatic charges. The electrostatic charges generated in underwear made from PVC fibres are, it is claimed, of value in the treatment of rheumatism. This is doubted by British and American clinicians.

Sorption Heat of Clothing Materials

The body is continuously liberating water vapour—the insensible perspiration—from the lungs and the skin. Textile materials, made by interlacing yarns spun from fibres, will allow water vapour to pass through the interstices of the fabric. In addition, many fibres, notably wool and other natural fibres, will absorb water; in doing so, they tend

18

to swell. The establishment of equilibrium between a hydrophilic fibre and the ambient air is, however, a slow process, particularly at low temperatures.

In 1858, the French military hygienist, Coulier, discovered that when dry fabrics absorbed atmospheric water vapour into their fibres (l'eau hygrometrique), there was a rapid and marked liberation of latent heat of condensation which caused a rise in temperature of the fabric. This effect was much greater in the case of wool than in the less hygroscopic cotton or linen. Coulier concluded that dry wool clothing had an anti-chilling or thermostatic effect (the heat sorption phenomenon) under damp-cold exposure or when the body was sweating profusely after exercise. This appeared to confirm the age-old idea that "wool next the skin" was a panacea for health and a prophylaxis against most diseases of the flesh, particularly rheumatism.

A suit of wool clothing of some five pounds weight can absorb about one pound of water vapour from the atmosphere; in doing so, it will liberate, for two or three hours, heat equivalent to the resting heat production of an average man. The importance of this effect is determined, however, by the amount of this free, intrinsic "central heating" that is available to counter effectively the heat loss from the body *inside* the garments.

In experiments carried out to study this effect, wool and "Terylene" (fibres of high and low moisture absorption respectively), of matched thickness and geometric construction, were made up into three layers of garments of the same design. The garments (underclothes, shirt, overgarments), suspended on clothes hangers, were instrumented at the three clothing layers with thermocouples, conditioned for 24 hours to a warm summer environment of 73°F (22·8°C) with a 30 per cent relative humidity, sealed in impermeable bags and exposed to the high relative humidity of 95 per cent at the same temperature. A rapid rise in temperature took place; in a quarter of an hour, the wool vest had warmed to 14·5°F (8°C) above the ambient temperature, and the "Terylene"

Fig. 7. The King of Westphalia, Napoleon's brother Jerome Bonaparte, and his consort. The queen is shown wearing a high-waisted, Empire-style gown modelled on pseudo-classical lines.

(From a painting by François Joseph Kinsoen (1771–1839), courtesy of the Musée de Versailles)

20

Fig. 8. An advertisement for the woollen combinations designed and advocated as a prophylactic cure-all by zoologist and physician Gustav Jäger (1832–1917). Use of his hair-odour pills, hygienic cigarettes and special chicory is also recommended.

vest had increased in temperature by about one half of this amount. The results of Coulier and the claims of wool scientists were thus confirmed.

The "clothes hanger" experiment was repeated with garments which were first conditioned to British, average winter room conditions of 68°F (20°C) and 40 per cent relative humidity, and then exposed to simulated, typical out-of-door British winter, damp-cold conditions of 40°F (4·4°C) and 95 per cent R.H. Cooling curves showed the temperature of the wool vest to be about 3°F (1·8°C) above that of the "Terylene" vest for about three hours. This less spectacular result on damp cold exposure is explained in part by the fact that vapour absorption into textile fibres is much slower at 40°F than at 73°F, hence the liberation of heat is retarded.

Fig. 9. This 4th century A.D. mosaic from Piazza Armerina, Sicily, indicates that the bikini is not so new a fashion after all.

(Photo: Alinari)

Statistically-designed physiological trials were carried out in a climatic chamber; men wearing the three layers of wool or "Terylene" garments were conditioned as before to the indoor winter conditions, and then exposed to the simulated out-of-door damp-cold environment. Surprisingly, no real (statistically significant) mean differences between the three layers of wool and "Terylene" garments were found, either in body skin temperatures or in temperature gradients between the garment layers. The thermostatic superiority of wool demonstrated in the physical model was not substantiated under fairly realistic physiological conditions. This may be explained in part by the fact that, under the conditions of damp-cold exposure, the relative humidity near the

22

warm skin is not at the 95 per cent ambient level but closer to 15 to 20 per cent; under these conditions, the absorption of water vapour is extremely slow. These experiments indicate that the practical significance of the thermostatic effect of wool (and probably leather) under cold-damp conditions is open to question.

Clothing Materials and Liquid Water

In general, fabrics made from fibres which have a high moisture vapour regain—particularly wool and viscose rayon —take up relatively large quantities of liquid water. As liquid moisture is absorbed, the fibres swell.

The absorption of liquid water may be influenced greatly by modification of the fibres, yarns or fabrics, e.g. by the application of finishes. Wool or cotton fabrics subjected to water-repellent varnish treatment, for example, may still absorb water vapour, but liquid water can no longer move readily into the interstices of the yarns and fabric.

The natural cuticle and surface waxes of wool exert a water-repellent effect which is especially noticeable in fabrics, such as Harris tweed, containing a high proportion of the coarser fibres. Wool garments, for this reason, may have a natural shower-resistance. In prolonged heavy rain, however, a dense wool greatcoat may eventually absorb double or more of its own weight of water, much of which occupies the interstices of the fabric.

Wool fabric can absorb into the fibres up to 40 per cent of its weight of water without feeling damp (i.e. there is little or no free water in the interstices of the fabric). Water is held within the fibres by physico-chemical forces, and it is given up more slowly than free water in the interstices. This explains why fabrics made from fibres which absorb only small amounts of water, e.g. many synthetics or specially-treated cottons, have "drip-dry" properties; the bulk of the water is held in the interstices of the fabric, from which it is readily removed.

Removal of Sweat

The absorption of water by fibres may be a disadvantage when fabrics are used in outer garments, but it is a valuable asset when fabrics are used in underclothing; it helps the underclothes to remove sweat from the skin.

Non-absorbent synthetic fibre fabrics take up water by a wicking process, the water (e.g. sweat) being held in the interstices of the fabric. It is widely believed that sweat-soaked garments of this type have a clammy feeling when worn next to the skin, and evaporation of the water causes chilling. Unabsorbed sweat retained at the body surface may be reabsorbed into the skin, blocking the sweat glands; it has been suggested that synthetic-fibre underwear (even in open-weave construction) may cause sweat rash and fungus disorders of the skin, particularly in humid, tropical conditions.

Experiments have been carried out to indicate whether or not synthetic fibre underclothes or nightwear (garments which actually touch the body) are, in fact, disadvantageous in this respect. The results are of particular interest to the soldier, explorer or mountain walker whose entire wardrobe may be represented by the pack on the back.

Wool socks, even if pre-shrunk, may still shrink and felt appreciably if washed without due care; they tend to develop holes, dry slowly and cannot withstand sterilization by boiling. For these reasons, trials were carried out by Army scientists in a desert area, to determine the relative hygienic value of traditional, grey wool socks and socks of "Terylene" of the same thickness and colour, and of matched weave geometry. Soldiers wearing the same type of boots used the two varieties of socks during several weeks of activity, including marches in the desert.

Analysis of the results showed no statistically-significant differences in boot or skin temperature, hygienic appearance of the feet, or in the incidence of fungus disorder of the toes (athlete's foot), as between one type of sock and the other. The sweat content of the "Terylene" socks, however, was

24

Fig. 10. Shillock woman wearing a buttock apron. Various parts of the body may be covered—or left uncovered—for reasons other than those indicated by European concepts of modesty.

(Photo by courtesy of the Ethnological Museum, Basle)

appreciably less than that of the wool socks, and the former dried much more rapidly after washing. Close examination of the data suggested that the "Terylene" socks wicked sweat from the foot and transmitted it to the inner absorptive surface of the boot leather by a process of "blotting", the flow of sweat being assisted by a mechanical pumping action resulting from movement of the feet during walking. The two types of socks were regarded as being equally comfortable.

The results of these experiments under desert conditions have been confirmed by extensive trials in many parts of the world. In consequence, the British Army, a very conservative institution, adopted "Terylene" socks for use by the soldier in all climates.

Results similar to those from the field trials were obtained in controlled laboratory experiments under simulated tropical conditions, using absorptive (viscose rayon) and non-absorptive (nylon) fibre underwear of a matched, close-weave construction. There were no significant differences between the two types of underclothing in respect of sweat remaining on the skin, total sweat loss, skin or internal body temperatures. There were no differences in the comfort of the garments when worn by people at rest, or during or after exercise. It is apparent, therefore, that synthetic (hydrophobic) fibre underwear of suitable weave may not display any particular physiological or hygienic disadvantages when worn under conditions of profuse sweating. An effective garb under these circumstances consists of an absorptive layer e.g. a cotton shirt, on top of the synthetic underclothes.

Wicking and a Wet Skin

Arguments against the use of non-absorbent, synthetic fibre underwear would apply with particular force to the use of these materials in baby clothes. The tender skin of the baby is

Fig. 11. Louis XIV's great-grandson in leading strings. Little boys were still being dressed in skirts in comparatively recent times and the custom may originally have been a means of outwitting the "evil eye".

(From an 18th century etching by J. Bonnart)

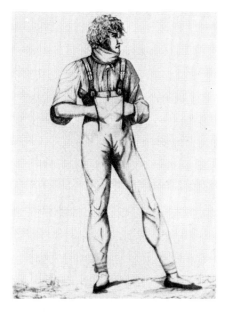

Fig. 12. The tight, high-waisted trousers and throat-constricting stock of the Empire fashion were described as "unhygienic" by contemporary physician L. J. Clairan. Tight clothing may produce sensations with a strong emotional overlay.

(Illustration from L. J. Clairan's "Recherches et considérations médicales sur les vêtements des hommes", Paris, 1803)

especially sensitive to constant exposure of the napkin area to irritating liquids. Trials have demonstrated that a water-impermeable sheet of rubber or plastic will keep the skin unduly damp and tend to cause a napkin rash; a synthetic staple fibre material of cellular weave, worn next to the baby's skin under a highly absorbent terry cotton (or viscose rayon) napkin, maintains a drier skin than do two terry cotton napkins used together. It would appear that urine wicks rapidly through the inner, non-absorptive fibre layer to blot onto the outer absorptive-fibre napkin, the flow of urine being aided, no doubt, by the vigorous movements of the baby's bottom. Since much of the liquid is absorbed into the outer cotton fibres, there is little tendency for it to wick back to the skin.

This technique of combining a non-absorptive synthetic-fibre material next the skin with an absorptive fibre outer layer is used in the Marathon (PVC) napkin, and in the nursing of incontinent bed-ridden patients.

27

Body Weight and Plastic Garments

It is generally recognized by clinicians that the Turkish bath is effective in invigorating people who already enjoy rugged health. As a way of losing weight, however, the value of the Turkish bath is minimal; sweating results in loss of water from the body, and this is replaced rapidly when the resultant thirst is quenched.

The principle of the Turkish bath is also applied in the form of moisture-impermeable, pliable, plastic sheet garments (for the trunk, limbs, waist, bust, neck, etc.), which are widely used in the hope of "melting away of unwanted fat easily, safely and without discomfort". Women are persuaded to wear such garments whilst carrying on their daily chores at home or out-of-doors, absorptive-fibre underwear being worn beneath the impermeable layer to take up the liquid perspiration. Under cool conditions, a portable "Turkish bath" treatment of this nature is of doubtful value, but can be regarded as relatively harmless. In hot weather, e.g. in the tropics, such impermeable garments may cause skin rashes, or even the suppression of sweating, with its consequent dangers.

6

TISSUES OF A SUIT

Garments are complex structures; they possess shape, drape and fit, and their physiological properties depend greatly upon other garments worn beneath and above them. The warmth of a clothing assembly derives from the combined thermal insulation values of its constituent fabrics, and those of the intervening layers of air. The effects of wind and liquid moisture are factors to be considered in assessing the comfort and warmth of clothing.

The conventional dress of the human male—shirt and tie, short jacket and trousers—became established about a century ago. It has now been accepted throughout the civilized world and, apart from the extravagances affected by ebullient youth, it seems unlikely to undergo any marked change in the foreseeable future.

A man's suit or overcoat has a complex anatomy which derives partly from the demands of fashion, and partly from the basic form dictated by convention. A man's jacket or coat generally has a lining, and between the fabric and lining is an insulating layer of air. Where drape is required (e.g. over the chest), interlinings are included. Pockets add extra layers. Shoulders and armpit areas are often heavily padded. The back of a jacket is often of a single layer of suiting, but the neck region, lapels and the anterior borders are self-lined. A waistcoat is built like a coat, but the back consists only of two thin linings. Thus, in a double-breasted suit, the demands of fashion provide extra insulation in the form of four layers of suiting, two interlinings and five air spaces over the front of the chest. Despite this, the front of a man's chest feels no

29

Fig. 13. An old Maori chieftain from New Zealand. Tattoos and scars, like ornamentation on clothing, may often be a sign of rank.

warmer than the back, except when he is out of doors in a wind. This is due to the fact that the skin adapts quickly to moderate differences in temperature, and it is more receptive to the average temperature of the trunk than to its parts.

It is clear that the "tog" value of a sample of fabric gives little indication of the overall warmth of a suit, particularly when this is worn with appropriate clothing on top and underneath. Some years ago, a full-sized copper manikin was developed by the American Army to measure the overall thermal insulation or "clo" value of cold weather clothing (one "clo" is equivalent to the overall thermal insulation of an average summer suit). The copper "man" is useful in that it enables scientists to carry out experiments which take account of the characteristic "body" shape of garments. On the other hand, it does not breathe or move, nor does it liberate insensible perspiration or liquid sweat, and the results of experiments must be assessed with this in mind. Two garments, for example, one of fibrous material and the other of a plastic sheet may have the same "clo" value as

Fig. 14. This comparison between a 17th century coat and its modern counter-part indicates that what is now non-utilitarian ornamentation may once have been a useful and necessary part of an everyday garment.

measured on a copper "man", but they will produce quite different physiological effects on a human man who is sweating profusely. Thus, the results of copper "man" experiments may be misleading. The same is true of the jointed aluminium "man" used for physiological studies of the astronaut.

In the case of both men and women, the trunk, with its relatively high skin temperature, is commonly covered with a minimum of three layers of garments. In every part of the world, however, and in all types of climate and weather, women cover the thighs, legs and feet—some 30 per cent of the skin surface—with gossamer-like stockings providing negligible thermal insulation. Chilblains of the feet, and poor circulation in the legs and thighs, are commoner in women

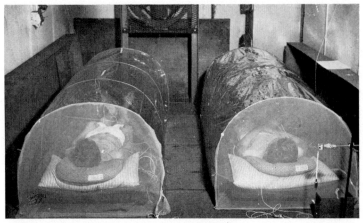

Fig. 15. Metallised film used as a light-weight blanket. Made into "tents" to encourage ventilation and minimise condensation of insensible perspiration, an unmetallised film is seen on the left and its metallised counterpart on the right. Mean results obtained in a designed experiment showed a higher skin temperature for the man under the metallised film.

than in men, and it seems likely that this results, at least in part, from the inadequate insulation properties of the female's nether garments. Young women, in particular, rely heavily on the thermal insulation provided by air spaces between thin garment layers, whereas the stronger sex still demands thicker materials which lie close together.

Air and water vapour permeability are often used in assessing the physiological properties of fabrics, but some of the body heat and vapour is transmitted through ventilation channels whose resistance is much lower than those of the weave interstices. A current of warm air, for example, flows upwards through the clothing to emerge at the neck; this is commonly described as "chimney ventilation". In cold weather, the neck opening may be closed by a scarf to minimize heat loss. In warm weather, removal of the tie will help to cool the body by allowing the currents of air to escape; the effect may be nullified, however, by the wearing of a

Fig. 16. Comparative tests of the "sorption" heat of hydrophilic and hydrophobic fabrics. Two men were used at a time, one wearing three layers of woollen and the other three layers of matched polyester fibre clothing of the same design. After equilibration to low humidity at a moderate temperature, the men were carried into a climatic chamber where the temperature was low but the humidity high. The cold junction can be seen between the two men and the globe thermometer above them.

fashionable cravat. Ventilation of this nature occurs also at the openings of sleeves and trousers, at the anterior edges and lower border of a loose jacket and overcoat, and around the tent-like bottom of a skirt; the flow of air is encouraged by body movements, or by a breeze.

33

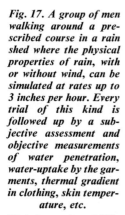

Fig. 17. A group of men walking around a prescribed course in a rain shed where the physical properties of rain, with or without wind, can be simulated at rates up to 3 inches per hour. Every trial of this kind is followed up by a subjective assessment and objective measurements of water penetration, water-uptake by the garments, thermal gradient in clothing, skin temperature, etc.

(*Photo by courtesy of "The Guardian"*)

Hats and Footwear

Hats are worn primarily for ornamental purposes; they are of only limited physiological importance. In conditions of extreme cold, however, hats prevent high heat loss through the scalp. They keep out rain, shade the eyes from the summer sun, and hide the bald male head from public view. It is doubtful whether thinning hair is related to the wearing of a tight fitting hat.

For centuries, pundits have proclaimed that good health is ensured by keeping the head cool and the feet warm. Shoes keep the feet warm, dry and clean, and protect the wearer from dirt and mud and from the irregularities of the ground.

Sandals and open shoes provide limited protection from the elements, but they have the virtue of ventilating the skin of the feet. Leather is a good absorber (but not necessarily a good transmitter) of water vapour. The impermeable adhesives sometimes used in the production of shoes can restrict movement of water vapour through the shoe substance. The dense leather of an outer sole absorbs liquid water very slowly; it is the seams of a shoe, particularly at the attachment of the sole, through which water tends to find its way. A good walking shoe has a fairly thick internal leather insole which is capable of absorbing water vapour or sweat. The inner surface of the shoe leather upper is also absorptive. This explains why no physiological or hygienic disadvantages have followed the introduction of the Direct Moulded Sole principle which has brought revolutionary changes in the

Fig. 18. Air permeability is determined by drawing air through a sample of fabric by means of a high speed vacuum pump. The pressure differential is controlled by a micromanometer and a rotameter measures the volume of air per second passing through the sample.

Fig. 19. The measurement of water vapour transmission through samples of cloth. The specimens being tested are covered by a permeable "guard" fabric and suspended over dishes containing water and an air layer of known depth. The differences in the weights of the dishes before and after 16 hours of rotation give the quantities of water vapour passing through a known thickness of air and each specimen.

footwear industry during recent years. A rubber or composition outer sole is welded directly to the leather upper, providing a non-leak seal and a long-wearing, water-resistant shoe or boot.

Research on military footwear has stressed that the sock must be regarded as an integral part of the shoe or boot. Socks are, for convenience in manufacture, fashioned usually in a symmetrical shape; this is of little consequence from the point of view of hygiene, unless the sock shrinks or is too small. Dense leather and rubber provide less heat insulation than an air-infiltrated and resilient knitted sock. With a tight-fitting boot, the warmth value of a very thick sock may be decreased because of compression; it can be unwise to use a removable insole or two pairs of socks (even of different size) unless the boot is sufficiently over-size. As long as a

Fig. 20. Resistance to penetration by wind is tested by placing a flat sample of fabric at right angles to the mouth of a wind tunnel. Uniformity of air-flow is ensured by honeycombs. The speed of the wind after it has passed through the sample is measured by a hot-wire anemometer.

(1) anemometer head, (2) air duct, (3) direction of wind, (4) honeycombs, (5) fabric, (6) recording apparatus.

(*Photo by courtesy of The Controller, H.M. Stationery Office. Crown Copyright reserved*)

"stretch", synthetic-fibre sock enables the toes to be freely moved, it has no particular disadvantages.

The design of a shoe is largely a matter of common sense. For a shoe to be a good fit, the toes must remain uncrowded and the front of the foot (particularly of children) must be given freedom to move and expand in the heat or with exercise. If the toes are free, as in an open sandal, the shape of the front of a shoe is of less significance. If shoes prevent the toes—especially the large toe—from maintaining a natural position (as in the case of the near-symmetrical, pointed Italian-style "winkle-picker" shoe) they can be expected to cause deformed toes, bunions and corns.

Some of the minor foot disorders commonly ascribed to badly-designed footwear used in early life may be, to some extent, inherited. A raised heel compensates for the short Achilles tendon which is said to be common in civilized communities; it is also claimed that raising the heel of the foot creates a position of muscular rest.

4

A 3-inch high heel makes for increased stature; it induces a hobbling, unstable gait of short steps; it makes the foot appear smaller than it is, and gives it an attractively-arched shape. The long, pointed women's shoe, on the other hand, exaggerates the length of the foot. High heels tend to rotate the pelvis in such a way as to accentuate the bust and flatten the stomach.

The validity of these contentions is a matter of debate; in any case, a woman's choice of shoes is seldom made with any regard to anatomical considerations. The principles that control the design of the modern woman's shoe derive less from the science of clothing hygiene than from the mysteries of feminine fashion and the magic of erotic symbols.

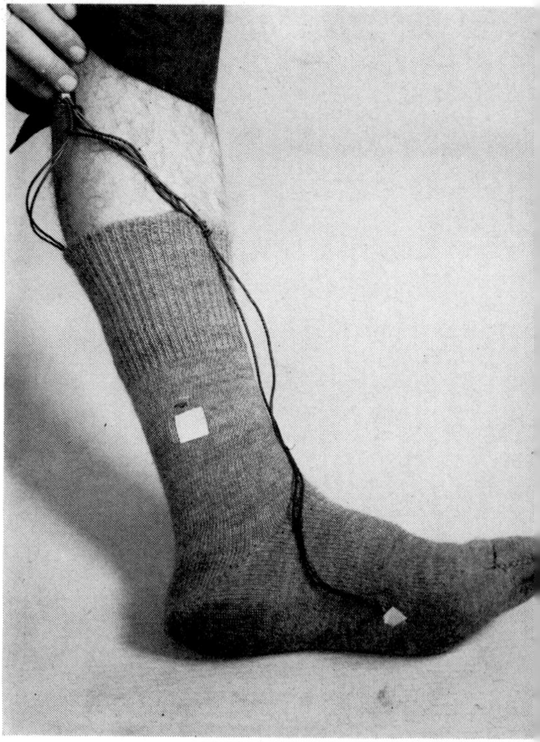

Fig. 21. The temperature o the skin of the feet, and of the leather insoles of boots or shoes, is measured at rest and during activity by means of gauze thermo-couple buttons. These cause no discomfort while walking. The wires are threaded through a sock to terminate in a plug.

7

CLOTHING HYGIENE

Clothing and Common Sense

Most people could, with advantage to health, become adapted to wearing lighter clothing, particularly in the warmer periods of the year. Women nowadays wear less clothing than their grandmothers, and appear to withstand the effects of partial nudity without undue distress. Women's clothing is usually lighter in weight than that of men. Thus a woman's shoe may weigh only a few ounces; a man's casual shoe, by contrast, will weigh two pounds or more, and a heavy walking shoe will commonly weigh four pounds. Weight carried by the feet represents expenditure of energy equivalent to at least twice that represented by a weight carried on the back; the weight of footwear is thus an important factor to be considered.

An average man's suit weighs four to five pounds, and a thick tweed suit weighs half as much again. A winter overcoat may weigh ten pounds or more. A man may carry a total load of more than a stone of clothing when outdoors in winter. This represents an appreciable load, and there is obviously much to be gained by wearing lighter clothes which can provide a similar degree of warmth and comfort. Under normal conditions, there are only insignificant differences in the physiological effects of outer clothing of similar construction made from different types of fibre, natural or man-made.

None of the widely-used modern fibres has any significant effect on the skin; some dyes and finishes, however, have been known to cause dermatitis in susceptible people. It is

39

always a wise precaution to wash new garments well before wearing them, particularly if they are to be worn next to the skin.

Hairy fabrics, especially those made from wool, may cause skin irritation in some people. Some medical authorities have suggested that an overwarm skin, mechanical irritation of a sensitive skin by hairy wool fabrics, and even a true allergy or sensitization to wool may play a significant role in certain cases of infantile and adult dermatitis.

Rainwear

Garments for keeping out the rain can be divided into those that are water-repellent or shower-proof, and those that are completely waterproof. The inherent water-repellency of coarse wool fabrics, such as Harris tweeds, has already been mentioned. Water-repellency may also be enhanced by the treatment of fabrics with agents which modify the surface tension characteristics of the material; protein products, waxes, aluminium compounds, silicones and pyridinium compounds are examples of water-repellent agents. Treatment of a fabric with such substances inhibits the absorption of moisture by the fibres and the wicking of water along the fibres and yarns. As the interstices of the fabric are not blocked, the transmission of air and water vapour through the fabric is virtually unimpaired. Many of these water-repelling agents are removed by washing and dry cleaning, and fabrics may need to be re-treated from time to time.

A shower-proof effect may also be obtained by constructing fabric in such a way that the yarns will swell when wet, closing up the interstices through which rainwater would find its way. This is the principle used in making "ventile" cotton fabrics. The fabric becomes shower-resisting, but remains permeable to air and water vapour.

In general, these methods of reducing the water permeability of fabrics by treatment with water-repelling agents, or by using "ventile" techniques, are effective to the extent that they enable the fabric to resist a reasonable amount of

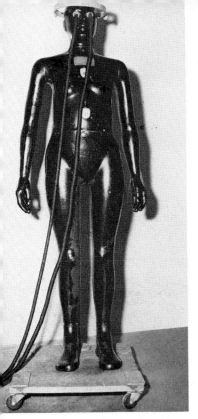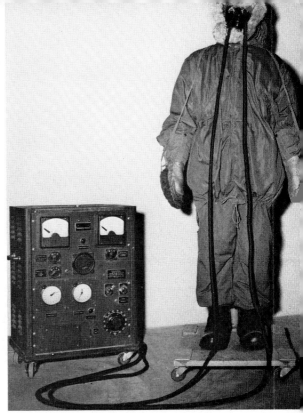

Fig. 22. The "Copper Man" used by U.S. Army laboratories to measure the insulating value of clothing assemblies and sleeping bags. Deficiencies traced with its aid are rectified before human subjects are employed to test clothing acceptability in the field.

(U.S. Army photo, courtesy of H.Q., U.S. Army Material Command, Washington, D.C.)

rain. They will seldom protect the wearer completely, however, from a really heavy downpour, especially in high winds. Water will eventually be forced through the fabric.

Complete resistance to water penetration is assured by sealing up the interstices in the fabric, e.g. with rubber or plastic, or by using sheets of rubber or plastic in place of conventional fabrics. Such materials are impermeable to water, and are regarded as "waterproof" rather than "shower-proof".

There is little to choose, physiologically, between the various forms of impermeable light-weight plastic or rub-

Fig. 23. Measurement of skin and rectal temperatures. The thermocouple elements are symmetrically placed in order to trace temperature variations between the two halves of the body. Contact between skin and elements must be gentle, as pressure may modify the underlying temperature. A mean skin temperature can be calculated from the readings obtained at the different sites.

(Photo by courtesy of The Controller, H.M. Stationery Office. Crown Copyright reserved)

berized raincoats. These garments are impermeable to air or water vapour, but if worn loosely they are ventilated adequately by currents of air created by body movements during walking. This ventilation, together with the cooling effect of rain, make the wearing of impermeable garments acceptable for short periods. Modern types of *microporous*, poromeric coatings are impermeable to water but permeable to water vapour. Rainwear made from these materials would seem to offer the advantages of the two types of material already described.

Waterproof rubber boots ("Wellingtons") usually have a thin absorbent lining and boots of this type are commonly worn with thick socks or stockings; between the two of them, lining and socks absorb much of the sweat produced, and allow a certain amount of air to circulate round the feet. During prolonged walking, however, ventilation is usually inadequate, and sweat accumulates inside such boots.

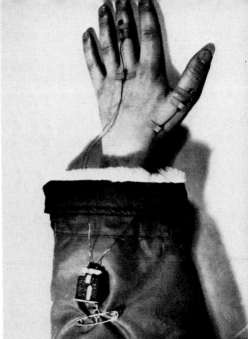

Fig. 24. Left: Simultaneous measurement of metabolism, pulse and body temperature. The man marching on a power-driven treadmill has a pulmonary ventilation volume meter in the pouch at his belt and a heart beat detector with transmitter in, respectively, his right and left hand breast pockets. Leads from skin and rectal thermocouples run down his left thigh. This combination of measuring devices is suitable for both field and laboratory work.

Right: When the temperature of the skin of the hand is being measured, thermocouple elements should be in firm but gentle contact with the skin. Here the subject is wearing cold-weather clothing and his hands will be covered with gloves during the experiment. He can be connected to the thermocouple circuit whenever required.

Textiles in the Hospital

Cross-infection in surgical wards is a problem associated with the use of textiles in hospitals. Research has shown that direct person-to-person transmission by infected nasal droplets is a less important source of cross-infection than is airborne dust. It was believed, at first, that much of the dust came from wool blankets, which can be difficult to sterilize without causing damage to the fabric. It now seems probable, however, that dust from cotton blankets or counterpanes

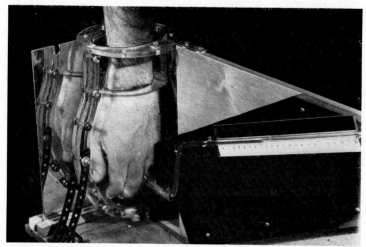

Fig. 25. Anatomical measurements of the hands help to develop gloves which give good thermal insulation but do not impair manual dexterity. Here a simple device is used to measure hand volume.

(Photo by courtesy of The Controller, H.M. Stationery Office. Crown Copyright reserved)

may be as effective as dust from wool in causing cross-infections. Cellular or terry blankets of cotton/viscose rayon blends, which do not shed particles readily, have been used with some success. It seems, however, that short of enclosing a blanket (or mattress) in a plastic bag, there is no way of preventing it from liberating particles into the air. One method of minimizing cross-infection resulting from such particles is to apply a wash-resistant antiseptic finish to blankets and other textiles used in surgical wards.

In this connection, there is evidence that germ-carrying airborne dust may arise from a patient's skin, as well as from the textile fibres of his bedding.

Highly-absorbent woven fabrics made from viscose rayon, alone or blended with other fabrics, are widely used in underclothes, babies' napkins, sanitary articles, hospital clothing and uniforms, bed sheets and surgical coverings, and in various forms of dressing (lint, gauze, bandages). In

44

the form of non-woven fabrics, viscose rayon is used as a man-made "cotton wool" or as sheets which can be sterilized by boiling. Non-wovens of this type can be treated with water-repellent finishes.

Several types of plastics are used in surgery for sutures, drainage tubes (polythene), artificial heart valves or blood vessels ("Terylene", silastic rubber) etc., repair of wounds (nylon lace mesh) and bone grafts (acrylics, fluorocarbons). During recent years, a great deal of attention has been given to the use of fabrics and films as surgical dressings. Calcium alginate fibres, for example, provide fabrics which are used in dentistry and surgery as absorbable, sterilizable dressings.

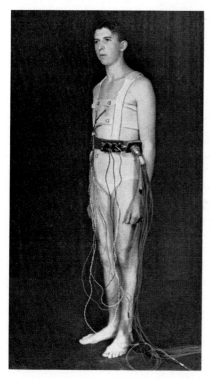

Fig. 26. Measurement of humidity or vapour tension at skin level. The humidity sensing elements are kept in firm but gentle contact with the skin by a harness and are connected by leads to a recording apparatus. Centred in a ring, each humidity sensing element consists of a polyvinyl alcohol film impregnated with lithium chloride as electrolyte.

Fig. 27. Wearing tropical dress, carrying equipment and stepping up and down a stool in time to a metronome in a simulated tropical environment, a soldier has his pulse rate, skin and rectal temperatures taken, and his sweat loss measured. Thermocouple leads can be seen emerging from the back of his collar. The man's subjective assessment of thermal comfort will be noted, and his underclothes and overgarments will be weighed separately.

(Photo by courtesy of The Controller, H.M. Stationery Office Crown Copyright reserved)

Clothing and Burns

Cellulosic fabrics, in general, will burn more readily than those made from protein fibres, e.g. wool or silk. Flammability is increased if the surface is raised or napped, as in cotton flannelette or wincyette, and materials of this type may be highly dangerous for certain applications, e.g. children's underclothing and nightwear. Flammability tests carried out on samples of cloth provide results which must be considered in relation to end uses. The thickness of material, the nature of linings and trimmings, the air spaces between clothing layers and, particularly, the design of the garment are factors which must be taken into account. A thin, loose, cotton nightdress is more likely to be caught up by flame from a nearby fire than a pair of pyjamas of the same material.

Blending provides an efficient method of reducing the flammability of fabrics. Some of the modern synthetic fibres,

46

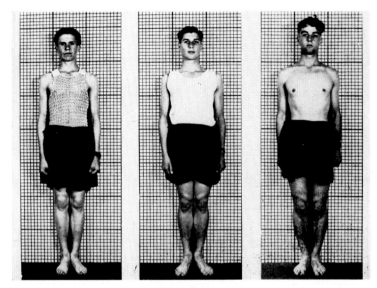

Fig. 28. In a statistically designed experiment, three men wore a string vest, a cotton vest, and "no vest" respectively under their otherwise identical clothing. At rest and when active under warm summer conditions, no significant differences were found between the three variables in skin and rectal temperatures, or in sweat loss. Only negligible differences were found between weight of sweat taken up by undergarments or outer garments.

notably modacrylic types such as "Teklan", and P.V.C. fibres such as "Rhovyl", may be blended with flammable fibres such as cotton to provide fabrics of low flammability.

At any one time, more than 500 people are likely to be in hospital in England suffering from serious burns; the majority of these are caused by clothes catching fire. The incidence of burns is ten times more common under the age of four than over the age of fifteen years.

Many types of "flame-proof" finishes have been used on fabrics in the past, often with only limited success. Some flameproofing agents, for example, are removed by washing.

"Proban" (an organic phosphate) and "Timonox" (an antimony compound) are examples of flameproofing agents

47

Fig. 29. The rapid pulse resulting from strain must be measured as soon as possible after exertion, as is being done here. Nowadays the heart rate is often measured automatically by transistorised apparatus.

(Photo by courtesy of The Controller, H.M. Stationery Office. Crown Copyright reserved)

used effectively for treatment of the clothing of children and the elderly. Both treatments tend to increase the weight and harshness of the material, and they add to the cost of the garments.

Nomex, a high-temperature-resistant nylon, is used in clothing that must not burn readily; it does not burn until temperatures of about 1500°F (815°C) are reached. Beta cloth, made from fine diameter glass fibre, provides fabrics which are completely non-flammable; it is used in making the space suits worn by Apollo astronauts.

Clothing on the Mind

European men have always preferred clothing that covers the chest and does not restrict the freedom of leg movement. Women, on the other hand, have opted periodically for freedom for the bosom—the "topless line"—and have favoured protecting the lower part of the body with heavy petticoats and skirts. Surprisingly, a nether undergarment covering the hips and thighs has been worn regularly by respectable women only during the last century.

In modern advertizing, textile fibres are accredited with all manner of attractive characteristics; cotton, for example, is "cool, calm, with a promise of inner warmth"; wool is "masculine and sexually attractive"; silk is "cool, sensuous and regal". These attributes are seldom related to any recognized physiological properties, but they are used effectively in creating an image for specific fibres.

Pattern and design are important factors in our assessment of clothing. A vertical stripe, for example, appears to accentuate height; horizontal lines give an impression of breadth. Hearing, likewise, plays a significant part in the sensory or emotional attributes of clothing. The click of high heels, the rustle of a dress or the sound of marching feet may stimulate a powerful emotional reaction in the sensitive listener.

Surprisingly, it is the male costume which retains vestigeal remnants, such as the lateral stripe of dress trousers, the functionless sleeve buttons, the unnecessary notch in the coat lapel and the bow in the headband of a hat.

Fig. 30. Goggles are meant to be a protection against dust and glare. Mounted on dummy heads next to a dust collector, two pairs are here being tested in the desert to determine penetration by dust. Objective measurements of visual acuity and colour vision were taken with men wearing lenses of different colours and tint intensities.

Throughout history, women have seized the opportunities presented by national crises, when the minds of men were otherwise engaged, to bring about revolutionary changes in feminine dress. These changes, usually transient, have become established as a part of modern life; they are now manipulated by the practitioners of fashion, and are the basis of a multi-million pound industry that controls the type of clothes worn by women throughout the world of western civilization.

INDEX